Hope, Healing, & Happiness After Divorce

Hope, Healing, & Happiness After Divorce

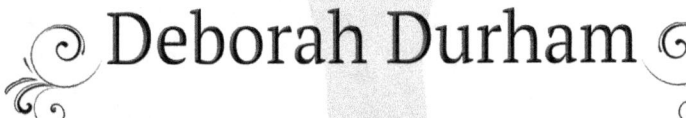

Deborah Durham

Hope, Healing, & Happiness
After Divorce

Copyright © 2016 Deborah Durham

All rights reserved. No part of this publication may be reproduced, stored in any retrieval system, or transmitted in any form or by any means, mechanical, photocopying, recording, or otherwise, without permission in writing from the publisher, except by a reviewer, who may quote brief passages in a review.

Cover and Interior design by Ted Ruybal

Manufactured in the United States of America

For more information, please contact:

Wisdom House Books
www.wisdomhousebooks.com
www.deborahdurham.com

Paperback ISBN: 978-0-9975573-0-5
Hardback ISBN: 978-0-9975573-2-9
EBook ISBN: 978-0-9975573-1-2
LCCN: 2016912236
FAM015000 FAMILY & RELATIONSHIPS / Divorce & Separation
REL012120 RELIGION / Christian Life / Spiritual Growth / Love & Marriage

1 2 3 4 5 6 7 8 9 10

Appreciation

I thank God for continually giving me grace and mercy each day!

Mom & Dad—To my mother who has gone on, who always encouraged me to do right even when the little girl in me just wanted permission to do wrong! She instilled great values in me. To my daddy who has gone on. All of your stories and words of encouragement still linger in my heart.

Chevon & Bria—You are the two smartest and most beautiful daughters in the world. I love you with all of my heart!

Bishop Cranford M. & First Lady Sandra B. Davis of Fresh Anointed Tabernacle Of Deliverance—Thank you for praying, believing, encouraging and supporting me daily as I learned who I was in the Lord. You both could always see past my faults, and acknowledged my needs.

Constance—To my lifelong friend, sister, and mentor, thank you for not giving up on me when I gave up on myself. Thank you for letting me be me!

Elder Henderson—Thank you for helping me to realize that God had a plan for me all that time and not to put my trust in man.

Joshua—Thank You! I often forget that you are only the age of 26. Wow! I Love You!

Last but not least, My Loving Husband—I thank God for not only your patience but for sending you to find me. May God continue to bless you!

Table of Contents

Foreword ix
Introduction xi
1. Deborah's Journey 1
2. The Divorce. 17
3. Voice of the Children. 23
4. Financial Independence 29
5. Hope and Healing 35
6. Journal to Freedom. 41
7. Loving Yourself. 51
8. Restoration 57
9. Moving Forward / Dating Again. 61
10. Joyful Living 67
11. What Caused Our Divorce? And How to Avoid It 71
12. Goals for the Future 81
13. Closing 87
14. Divorce Manual. 89
Resources 121
About the Author. 122

Foreword

Friends first. How many times have you heard this? What happens when your best friend becomes your husband, the father of your children, and then your ex husband? How do you pick up the pieces and move forward after divorcing your best friend?

Deborah Durham, takes you through this heart wrenching experience in her book, *Hope, Healing, and Happiness After Divorce.*

She describes her experiences before, during, and after her divorce.

She offers scriptures and resources to help individuals who may be going through a divorce. Having gone through a divorce myself, I truly wish books and resources such as this were made available to me.

I have known Deborah for over twenty years. She has a genuine love for people. Her passions are reading, writing, and being an advocate for children.

I believe Deborah was inspired by God to tell her story in this book, to encourage someone who may be going through this dark time in their life.

This book is a must read. It's all about healing and moving forward.

—Constance H. Davis

Introduction

This book was written to heal men and women who have experienced separation and divorce in their lives, as I have. It's my wish that it will be a resource and tool for helping individuals to get back on track and to provide an open door to forgiveness and healing.

While in some scenarios divorce is imminent, others may hold the possibility of hope. Every marriage will have its share of ups and downs; as long as God is your foundation, and there is hope, you should continue to strive for success. I'm a Christian and truly believe that if it wasn't for God, I would not have been able to handle all of the stresses that came with my divorce. I reference God many times throughout the book. You may have different beliefs or call God by a different name.

When writing this book, here are a few questions that came to mind. What happens when a marriage ends in divorce? Who is affected? How can families move on? These are just a few of the questions I've been faced with over the last few years since I divorced from my husband of eleven years.

Many women show affection often, versus some men who rarely show affection. Those women tend to hold on to situations a lot longer than most men, bottling up the emotions inside of themselves. As a result, some women may eat, drink, shop, read or even withdraw from others to cover up the hurt, also known as a coping mechanism. Many times this causes us to holler out of our natural voices, no longer being able to keep those feelings inside. But when we ask the Lord to release all of the hurt that has been bottled up inside, we can finally begin to heal from the pain. The Lord knows every tear we have cried and every hair that is on our head. Until we scream, cry, and let go of all the pain, we cannot truly move on. We must release all of the hurt, bitterness, jealousy, unwillingness to forgive, strife, envy, and malice that is in our hearts. After this is released, we can move on to the healing process.

Prayer For You

This is my prayer for each of you as you take your precious time to read
Hope, Healing, and Happiness After Divorce.

Dear Heavenly Father, Lord, I pray for each person who has found him or herself in divorce, and ask that you continue to heal and deliver them as they read this book. Please remove the layers of hurt, guilt, shame, embarrassment, disappointment, and loneliness. We admit our mistakes so we will be able to start this new chapter in our lives. As they begin to rediscover who they are in Christ, use this opportunity to rebuild each individual self-esteem and self-worth. Let each person know that you have the plans already mapped out for them; all they need to do is trust you and have faith that you will provide for their every need. I thank you for the change in their hearts, the testimony they will receive and the message they will one day be able to deliver to another in need. We trust, believe and honor you.

In Jesus' name, Amen!

Chapter 1

DEBORAH'S JOURNEY

God grant me the serenity to accept the things I cannot change, courage to change the things I can, and the wisdom to know the difference.
—Reinhold Niebuhr

There are two sides to every story. As I reflect, I ask myself, what happened? What part did I play in this divorce? What does God want me to learn from this situation? Lord, please allow me to receive what you are teaching me through this journey.

After being married, for the second time, I ended up in divorce. How could . . . Why would . . . this happen to me again? At the age of forty-seven, with two beautiful daughters, by two different "boys" . . . Ugh. I never in my wildest dreams expected my second marriage to end. "Lost for words" is the best way I can explain it.

Being the fifth of six children, I always felt like a loner in my family. It was like I was that piece of the puzzle that couldn't quite find its place. That was not easy, especially in such a huge family. At the age of sixteen, I had my first child due to my own bad decisions. I was hurt and was looking for someone to fill the void in my life (all I really needed was God but I did not realize it at the time).

Even though I attended church regularly, I didn't have the relationship with God I should have had. I did not read positive words daily or pray daily. Growing up, it was mandatory that our family had to go to church every Sunday, including Sunday school, choir rehearsal, etc. I'm sure many of you can relate to this. I just went to church because that was what my family and I thought was right. You know, traditions! At that time, I had no clue how important having a solid foundation would offer up a clear direction in my life; I was in preparation. Preparation is a powerful commodity. In my opinion, God has the ability to take you places that you may not understand or fathom in your mind at that very moment. However, it's preparing you for your future endeavors. Not that it will come easily, or without challenge. It sets you up for your future promises. He also gives us the freedom to make our own decisions. It's called free will. Looking back, I feel as though I should have made better choices. However, those choices did provide preparation for what was to come.

Because I had my first born so young, I endured the disappointment from my family, especially because I was having a baby out of wedlock. Back in my day, that was a big "no-no." I didn't realize it, but God was shaping and molding me into the person he needed me to be. He turned my "mess" into a "message." Even when we make mistakes, God is right there. He knew our choice before we did. Out of this situation, I received a beautiful blessing, my daughter.

My first born's dad was charming, popular in school, and easy on the eyes. I felt special when he showed me attention; there were so many other young ladies who admired him, but he chose me. At least that's how I felt. I was with him for all the wrong reasons. Once I told my parents that I was pregnant, they quickly ended the relationship. Not before my sister jumped on him and made it very clear that he was never to come back around. She is the firecracker in our family, to say the least. We love her. Needless to say, the relationship with my baby's father did not work out.

After that, I began dating the man who would become my second born's father, who was my best friend, and high school sweet heart. For the sake of his privacy, we will refer to my best friend as "Max." We dated on and off again from ninth grade of high school through college. People used to look at us and say that we would always be together. We were best friends. When you saw one, you saw the other. I even joined the track team and volleyball team to be closer to him. He played football and that took up a lot of his time. In hindsight, he was the reason I became a teacher. Yes, he actually chose my career. He told me I needed to be a teacher and that this was my calling. At the time, he saw something in me that I didn't see in myself.

I'm thankful for my parents because they gave me no other option but to attend college. When choosing a college, of course, I wanted to be close to Max, so we enrolled in the same school. Things finally came to a halt in college after I stumbled upon him cheating. This wasn't the first occasion he cheated in our relationship. I went to Max's apartment and there was an impressionable young lady sitting in my boyfriend's bedroom. I was stunned, with an expression of concern and horror on my face. My heart felt as if it would jump out of my chest. She immediately informed me that she was his girlfriend. After a short conversation with this young lady, she left and I stayed there trying to make sense of the situation. Max and I got into a huge argument, that I'm sure anyone within a mile of the apartment heard. He acted as though it was just an innocent situation.

God sends hidden messages to us, and it is best to stop and take note of these things. Perhaps we would prefer to maintain a blind eye. However, failure to recognize and understand these messages could lead to a buildup, like a brick wall that will stop you in your tracks. Each failure to recognize a message is like a brick being molded into a seemingly unbreakable wall. Catching the young lady at Max's apartment was my "brick." When we are in love with someone who doesn't love us enough, often times the signs are there, but we ignore them because we want so much for the relationship to work. However, we have to learn to sit still, be quiet, and listen to what God is trying to tell us. Otherwise, we may miss out on our blessings, because we are trying to shape life into the way we will have it to be and not how God purposed our lives. God has a beautiful way of reminding us that we are not in control, yet He is.

After breaking up with my high school sweetheart in college, it took a lot of time to heal. Sometimes we think we have healed from a situation only to learn that there is more healing to do. My heart was shattered into a million pieces. I couldn't imagine life without him. He was my right hand, my best friend, my first true love, my knight in shining armor. I was devastated, hurt, disappointed, and once again feeling affectionately lonely.

A few years later, I met my first husband. The marriage lasted only three months. Yep, that's right, three months. There was an age difference that I believe affected us. He was much younger. He loved partying and I was more of a home body. The saying "opposites attract" was true in this relationship. We dated for a year. We were two young adults enjoying life. We married, and I quickly realized that I had made the wrong decision when I had trouble finding him at our reception (another "brick"). I knew immediately there was a big problem. He dealt with a lot of hurt and pain from his past, and I truly believe he thought the marriage would fix it, or at least cover it up.

I have to ask myself, what was my motive for getting married at the age of twenty-five? Part of me wanted to be married by a certain age because my co-workers thought it was necessary by that age. I will never forget how they kept after me week after week, month after month, about getting married. In my heart, I knew I wasn't ready to be married, but once again—traditions! I thought this was the age that I was supposed to be married, based on society's belief. It's like we have our lives mapped out on how it should go day to day, year by year. But sometimes, things don't go as planned. Before I knew it, I was filing for divorce. I didn't realize it at the time, but I never really healed from my relationship with my high school sweetheart. I was feeling lonely after the divorce and wanted to bury my pain. So, I set out to find "him," the one, my knight in shining armor, by any means necessary. He was my "best friend" in high school, yes, the one who had hurt me several times. Yet, I still loved Max unconditionally; my heart yearned for him, and I wanted to pick up where we left off. He stayed on my mind night and day, and soon I tracked him down and eventually married him.

When we reconnected, he was happy to see me as well, but I know now that this was not ordained by God. I received his number from a friend. We spoke a few times over the phone and ended up meeting at a store to reunite. It was refreshing to see him after being apart for so long. My heart was beating so fast. I was anxious, excited, and had butterflies in my stomach. He looked amazing. He was happy to see me, and we both acted as though nothing bad had ever happened between us.

The problem here was that I found him, but I should have remained true to my deep roots and traditions, that is, that the man should find his wife. "He who finds a wife finds a good thing," (Proverbs 18:22-NKJV). I think when a man seeks a woman the traditional way by chasing after her, it demonstrates how much love he has for her. It allows the woman the comfort of knowing that her man sees the value in her. That she is worth pursuing. Ladies, always remember your values, and never allow anyone to treat you in less of a manner than you deserve. It's important for both men and women to understand that we are valuable beyond measure and should always be treated as such.

We had a wonderful courtship, but I knew he wasn't in it for me. After all, I was the one that pursued him. Looking back, I know that he didn't love me enough. I should have allowed him to demonstrate how much he valued me by allowing him to pursue me.

We began dating again, and after some time, he asked me to marry him. It wasn't a traditional romantic request, which I would have loved considering all that we had been through up until this point. However, I married him anyway. After marrying, we began raising two beautiful daughters together. I loved him unconditionally; the best I knew how. I would plan trips each year to ensure that we spent quality time together and also planned some trips with the girls. He was a hard worker and it was hard to pull him away from work.

He was a great family man but he never attended church with us. I understand now that not having the same traditions and values can really take a toll on a marriage. It makes it harder when you don't have some of the same principles. If anything, please take away from this book the importance of discussing the foundation of your marriage, which should include respect, trust, compassion, and values, especially as they pertain to God. It was a struggle getting him to come to church. He felt that church people were doing the same things as worldly people. He saw individuals who held titles in church out with women, drinking, gambling, etc. He didn't understand why he should fellowship with hypocrites. I tried to encourage him to understand that not all church people were this way, because it was important to me that we attend church as a family. No one is perfect, and everyone always has room for growth. This is why we have such an important role in society because we never know who's watching us. Even though he didn't go to church, he was attentive to church members and their role in society.

He came from a great family, and I did too, but we were not marrying our families; we were marrying each other. Our marriage lasted for eleven years. It was not perfect, but we made it work. Looking back, it felt like we lived together but had our own lives. He did what he wanted to do, and so did I. I cooked occasionally, more like every blue moon, but we ate out a lot. I paid all of the large bills and he paid the small ones. It was more like a partnership than a marriage.

During the last years of our marriage, he had an affair with a young lady that he denied over and over. I first learned about her when she called my home at 1:00 in the morning. She wanted to be sure I knew that she had been with my husband. I tried to convince myself that she was just a disrespectful person who was trying to cause trouble with my family. She called our home many times and used vulgar language. She even showed up to our home and threw his clothes all over our front lawn. Even through this, I stayed and I still believed him.

I had been praying for weeks for God to let me know if my husband was cheating in our relationship or if I was just being jealous for no reason, even though the answer was already there. One late night, it became perfectly clear for me. His mistress called and told me things only he could have told her about our marriage throughout our years together. For over an hour, she told me the things he didn't like that I had been doing in our marriage and so much more. He told her that I wasn't cooking or cleaning, and that I was not attractive. It's amazing how some women (or men) feel as though they have the "magic touch" and can float into your life, snatch your husband (or wife) and live happily ever after with "your man" (or woman). She told me that she didn't know that he was married at first, but by the time she found out, it was too late. Her feelings were too involved, and she couldn't let him go.

Somehow, I remained strong and didn't break down like I wanted to over the phone with her. The fact that I wasn't upset actually made her more upset. When I love, I love with everything in me, so I was hurting but felt that it was important that I hold it together one moment at a time. During our conversation, I tried to explain that we started dating at the age of sixteen and I basically knew how he "ticked." She had been with my husband for some time; how much time I truly will never know. But she didn't know him like I did. As I listened to her, I began to think about all of the things she told me and started putting together a timeline in my head of different events. For starters, it all made sense that he no longer wanted me to come by his job. That was where they met. She would frequently visit his job; according to her, she stayed very close by. She said they went to very nice restaurants on a weekly basis. This explained why he would get home so late. Max told me that all of a sudden he had big workshops going on at his job. Which he never had before. Let's just say I had a "light bulb" moment. The light went on and provided a spot light on all of the things my heart never wanted to see, but my mind already knew. Provision was made to clear the air, and identify the truth, as painful as it sounded.

After this light bulb moment, I continued to ask him several times about saving our marriage, but he continued evading the question, simply telling me he would let me know soon. He said things like, "Let's talk about it later," or, "This is not a good time," or, "Give me until June." Soon never came, but June did and I had to make a decision because my heart was so heavy and in so much pain. What a trying time in my life! God had answered my prayers and now it was time for me to make a choice, because I could no longer be blind to what was going on. My life, and most importantly, my children's lives were at stake. Our youngest daughter took it the hardest. She began to act out in school and her grades went down. Things were no longer the norm. She was tempted to join a gang in school, when she was in the seventh grade. I believe she was around twelve years old at the time. Her entire demeanor changed; she didn't want to talk to family anymore. She began hanging with new friends that had a negative influence on her. I was devastated and felt she blamed me for everything that occurred in our marriage.

It was not an easy road. My self-esteem hit rock bottom. I was always told how beautiful I was outwardly, but it certainly didn't feel that way inside. I had given power over me in this situation. We lived apart for several years due to yet another relationship, which he denied over and over again. Unfortunately, I continually received calls from another woman who would curse me out fearlessly. This was unnerving, and I often feared for my children's safety, and mine–one of the scariest moments a mother can go through. I didn't know who this woman was; she called me from private numbers constantly. I didn't know anything about her, but it felt as though she knew everything about me. It was truly an alarming time. I would always wonder, when I was out at the grocery store or at the mall shopping, if she was a few steps away. I didn't know what she looked like or what she was capable of at that time. Although she continued calling and harassing me (several "bricks"), I stayed in denial. I pretended that this was just a really bad dream. I didn't want to know the truth nor did I want to accept the truth. There were signs all around me and yet I still didn't want to believe it. I prayed constantly, asking God to reveal to me if my husband was cheating on me, even though he had shown me over and over. I wanted undeniable proof and he gave it to me time and time again.

One day, I woke up and decided a change must occur. The relationship we held on to was not healthy for our daughters or for us. He would visit anytime he wanted. He ate with us, watched television with us, laid on my bed, kissed and hugged us anytime he felt like it. Sometimes he would even sit in the den all alone watching TV. I couldn't understand how he could live a double life and show no emotion. Why didn't he understand the hurt and pain that he was causing? Some days I felt as though I couldn't breathe; as though I was suffocating and no one could see me. Finally, I decided enough was enough. God gave me a choice and I filed for divorce and asked for total custody of our daughter. He signed the papers and there I was . . . Free again. Even though he loved the girls, I needed to feel closure from our relationship. I believe he was okay with giving me custody of the girls because he didn't want to make things any harder for them than it already was, based on the changes he began to see in them.

I felt so relieved the day of the divorce. I could finally begin to put this all behind me. I ate breakfast with a friend, went back to work and seemed to hold it all together. The next day, I cried on and off all day after telling my Pastor I was emotionally okay. I thought I would have closure after the divorce, but it wasn't closure and it really hit me hard. It was bitter sweet. I was on an emotional roller coaster ride. I had a lot of support. My friend went with me to lunch and tried to encourage me as much as she could. During this season of my life, I also lost my dad, got a new job I did not want, joined a new church and my daughter was attending a new school. It felt like it was too much for me, but I kept remembering that God would never let us down and he would never put more on us than we could bear. So, as sad and disappointed as I was, I decided that I must go on.

Losing my dad was a very painful experience in and of itself. He was a very important part of my life. I looked up to him, depended on him, and valued his opinion. He was the person here on earth I counted on to help me get through life's challenges. He shared priceless wisdom that will remain in my heart for a lifetime. He was my rock. We often shared words of the Bible daily and how to use them in life experiences. He was always very transparent and would share his own personal experiences as a testimony of how good God was to him.

Even though time has passed, I am still in the healing process daily. I struggle with the failure of it all and sometimes feel rejected. I still have trouble with the word "divorce." When anyone discusses it, I sometimes feel ashamed and really uneasy during the whole conversation for different reasons:

1. **I feel my daughter still blames me for everything that happened in the relationship.**

She began spending more time alone in her room. We no longer ate together or did things together.

2. **I feel like I'm hiding behind layers and layers of emotions and past events.**

I never liked sharing my feelings with anyone. When I was growing up, we were always told not to discuss things that were going on in our home. Therefore, it's hard for me to share personal information with others.

3. **I am now in a new relationship. Because I don't want to get hurt, it is sometimes hard for me to be fully vulnerable with him and let my emotions out.**

It isn't fair to him when I don't share how I feel. It can sometimes hinder us from connecting as we should.

Through everything, God's love and comfort has helped me to feel less shame and guilt. But most importantly, He has shown me where I need to grow and that I myself had a part in this divorce.

New And Lonely Beginning

After the divorce, I kept trying to find someone I could talk to and confide in. Fortunately, I found a confidant in one of my closet friends. She listened and did not criticize either of us for our individual shortcomings in the marriage. She understood that this man was not just my husband, but also my "best friend." Talking to her helped a little, but it seemed that I still didn't really have someone to turn to. I felt it was hard for her since she knew us both pretty well, and sometimes she didn't believe what I shared based on her friendship with him. She heard what I was saying, but it was hard for her to believe it because she knew him, too. So, I finally decided to try God, and it ended up being exactly what I needed! As I began building a closer relationship with God, I realized that all of those tests and trials only came to make me strong.

My relationship with Him didn't become perfect overnight. I still have a lot of work to do. Building a relationship takes time and effort. You have to study your word daily. Sometimes just sitting in a room quietly and dwelling in his presence was all I needed. My Bishop often says, "If God is not working on you; he's working on your situation." Some answers only come through prayer, fasting, and meditation on his word. Also, having the ability to utter the Lord's word is key to your healing.

During family gatherings and work functions, surrounded by all kinds of people, I still felt alone. I've always felt different and even at the age of fifty, I felt set apart as a person in this world. It was as if I was physically there, but invisible at the same time, even though I clearly wasn't. I would try to talk with people and it seemed as if they were avoiding me everywhere I turned. So I started challenging God, crying out to him in the midst of each gathering I attended. Saying . . . Lord, can you hear me? Where are you? Why is this happening to me? Why do I feel invisible? No one will talk to me or hear me. When he answered, He said that sometimes He just wants to speak to us alone. So I tried to listen but I was still upset, and everyone else seemed to be having so much fun! I remained encouraged, seeking God on a daily basis, asking for strength to get through.

Chapter 2

THE DIVORCE

And who of you by being worried can add a single hour to his life?
(Matthew 6:27- NASB)

Divorce is a legal separation of a man and a wife; a breaking of ties within a marriage. I have spoken with many couples who are in their second or third marriage who continue to struggle. It's truly a day-to-day process.

What do we understand about divorce today? For some of my friends that are divorced, this is a hush-hush subject. The unspoken rule of thumb is to never discuss it. It's the white elephant in the room. I challenge you to discuss it. How can you heal or help someone else if you never exchange your personal experiences in life? Depending on your religious belief . . . some believe that divorce is completely forbidden. Some do not believe in remarrying. I personally believe that when there is adultery in a marriage, or the loss of a spouse, God gives us permission to remarry.

Many individuals may divorce and never recover financially or emotionally because of the stigma behind divorce. I have news for you! There is life, hope, healing, love, and happiness after divorce.

A little girl's dream is to walk down the aisle with beautiful garments, family and friends to adore her. Sometimes this focal point can take our minds off of what's really important, which is laying down a platform to ensure a successful marriage as best you know how. I never thought our marriage would end in divorce with so many harsh feelings. I thought we would be happy. This sad heartbreak happened to us. We both felt betrayed, hurt. We felt bitterness and resentment toward each other. These emotional feelings stayed with us during and after the divorce. I had no idea how to pick up the pieces, along with all the bills left on me from the marriage and children to take care of by myself. Divorce is one of the most painful experiences because I am still alive but it felt to me as though a death had taken place in my life. I had to do things in my life as well to be emotionally free again.

Here are some things that I had to do to get through the divorce:

- Grieve the marriage. I cried a lot and vented all my frustrations to the Lord and close friends.

It's okay to feel hurt, but you have to remember that it will pass.

- I also felt the need to write a letter to my ex-husband and vowed to burn it. I did everything that I could to get rid of the hurt. I knew I struggled with issues of bitterness and a lack of forgiveness.

The letter was a way to share exactly how I was feeling at that time; hurt and disappointed, just to name a few. I was able to truly express myself with transparency without hurting him in the process. "Above all else, guard your heart, for everything you do flows from it," (Proverbs 4:23). I did not want my heart to be hardened toward him or other people in my life. The letter was a release for me.

- My trustworthy friend gave me a safe place sometimes to rest my head and to get away from others. She also just listened to me when all of the drama was too much to handle.

Find someone you can trust with your heart. That you're able to speak to freely without feeling judged or discouraged.

- I learned to cry out to the Lord and be honest with not only Him, but myself as well, about how I was truly feeling on the inside. It was helpful for me to share with the Lord what I was going through. I asked Him to forgive me for another mistake I had made in my life.

The process of forgiveness was long and hard for me, but I made it through. I didn't realize the amount of strength and courage I had within myself. No matter what you do in your life, God still loves you. Something happened to my heart in the process. I was not only able to forgive someone that was close to me but to love again as well. I could not let this divorce be the end of my story or my life. I had to forgive so I could be free again.

If you are still struggling with seeing your ex-spouse, you have not moved on.

Signs of struggling:

- Feeling Anxious or Uncomfortable when hearing or talking about him or her.
- Not wanting to be in the same room.
- Blaming everything on him or her.
- Angry with him or her, etc.

Just because he or she is out of sight does not mean that you are truly free.

Remember that this will be an "emotional roller coaster" ride, because people are emotional creatures. I had happy days, sad days, angry days, lonely days and the list goes on. Try to be mindful that you were not the only individuals involved in this marriage that didn't quite make it. There will be family members and friends who are hurt by whatever took place in this thing called marriage which brought about many relationships. So try to remain positive. Others did not live or experience your journey. Choosing to remain positive is highly recommended because stress can wear and tear on your body, emotionally and physically.

When you finally decide to pursue your divorce, you must remember what is best for all parties involved. I first had a free consultation with a local lawyer in my city.

Here are a few things to know about divorce:

- Money can play a big part.
- Time is important because you have to wait a year before divorcing.
- Legal advice is key to protecting yourself.

Due to the cost factor, I decided to get a legal advisor, which was much cheaper, and I represented myself. I was very fearful during the whole court experience. There are so many details that you should make sure are covered in the agreement before you proceed to court. In our marriage we had children, houses, cars, and land. When the advisor and I first wrote up the divorce decree, we only asked for total custody of the children. I was so anxious to get the divorce; I neglected to include the house. He did sign and agree to the request. Years later, I was still in the house we lived in with the precious antiques trying to get his name off the title because he refused to sign. The divorce was cheaper but still left so many things unsolved. This is the major reason I wish I would have paid money to be represented by a lawyer. Now, I have to hire a lawyer to finalize all of our assets, which should have been done before our divorce.

My ex continues to be bitter and not communicate with me at all, which can make the process a little bit harder when trying to move forward. Sometimes he will not speak until almost made to by family members. Here are some of the things he shared with me at one point.

#1. I would not even make it a week without him and #2. I would not move on with my life. We have to rebuke these feelings of hurt that our significant other may try to speak over our lives. I try to remember that we are all different individuals and the healing process can take longer for others. I have to respect that, so I continue to pray for him and his healing.

I did file for child support with our local Department of Social Services. This was done during our initial separation, and I was told by a lawyer not to change it for any reason during our divorce. I felt that the amount of money I received weekly from him to cover all of the monthly expenses was unfair. There is a formula to decide how much child support you will receive. One of the criteria involved my job salary, and I made just about the same salary as he did yearly, so that was not to my advantage. I was anxious to get all of this behind me; therefore, I made several mistakes.

Mistakes when representing myself in court:
- I didn't include the house.
- I didn't ask for alimony.
- I didn't request help with college tuition.

My wish is that through my testimony, this will help you if you are separated or in the middle of a divorce.

Chapter 3

VOICE OF THE CHILDREN

Behold, children are a gift of the Lord, the fruit of the womb is a reward. (Psalm 127:3- NASB)

Through the separation and divorce process, my eldest daughter was very strong, determined and opened-minded. She has always been willing to enjoy life to the fullest, loving God, people, and herself no matter what. With my ex husband and I, she continues to be very supportive and encouraging, never choosing sides. I do believe she was upset about the divorce and separation, but still wanted us to feel loved. Her kind heart made it possible for us to attend her wedding ceremony and reception together. It was great sharing in their special moment, our new son-in-law was a delight, and a welcome addition to our family. She always worked on helping the family stay together, as a whole, in love and unison. While my older daughter seemed to be coping well with the divorce, my youngest daughter was going through a different experience.

My youngest daughter struggled in school due to the separation and divorce. She attended at least ten teen counseling sessions at her school but was unwilling to share her thoughts or feelings with the counselor. So the counselor and I thought it was better to cancel the sessions due to the cost and lack of response from her. We've always attended a Bible-based church and she was involved in other activities that helped her get through the day. Some of the activities included the Praise Dance Ministry, sewing club, honor guards, etc. She had little contact with her father unless it was a holiday. During their time together, he enjoyed buying her gifts or taking her out to eat. I never felt very comfortable with him taking her from my presence while she was a youth or teenager, so their visits were often very short. However, I now realize that having them spend time together was vital to our kids' healing.

Here are a few recommendations for helping your kids cope with divorce:

- **Communicate with your kids.** Please use discretion. You know your kids and if they are able to handle what you are about to share with them. However, for those that are mature enough to handle it, don't be afraid to have those difficult conversations with them. We are afraid of how our kids will feel if we tell them what is truly going on in our marriage. However, sometimes we should be more afraid if we don't tell them. Kids are pretty smart and they can figure things out on their own. We don't want them to consider the advice of coping from their friends who are less experienced. It's better to hear it from their parents.

- **Try to stay positive around them.** They can sense when you're hurt or something's wrong. So try to keep things as normal as possible, under the circumstances. They need reassurance that things will be okay. Sometimes just hearing you say that to them will lift their spirits.

- **Keep them busy with extracurricular activities.** It's so important to maintain their day-to-day structure. When they are busy with activities they have less time to think about what's going on at home. They can focus their attention on positive reinforcements. Most importantly, keeping busy is a great stress reliever.

- **Always remember that they are watching you to see how you handle each situation.** You are their biggest role model. They are going to mimic what they see you do. Therefore, don't have the philosophy, "Do as I say, not as I do." Trust me, whether they want to or not, many times kids will grow up and follow in the same footsteps as their parents, even making the same mistakes as their parents.

As difficult as it was for me to stay positive, it was the best thing to do for everyone involved. This helps with a lot of the communication issues, difficult conversations and disagreements that may often occur. So always try to stay positive with your ex, even when it feels impossible. He or she will always be a part of the family if there are children involved. Continue to communicate about your child's progress in school, activities and anything else they may be involved in. Remember, if it were not for him or her, you would not have those precious gifts—your children.

Children don't come with manuals, so the role of a parent or guardian can be a difficult one. We often raise our children the way we were brought up, but sometimes the best way is to rely totally on God for help.

My youngest daughter still has a lot of questions about the divorce:

- What happened?
- Could you have done anything different?
- Did you forgive my dad?

Questions she had at the time of the Divorce:

- Why do you have to divorce? Can't you work it out?
- Can we continue to live together?

We both developed low self-esteem but are improving daily because of the wonderful people that are now involved in our lives. For me personally, I did not always like pictures of myself, or looking in mirrors. I felt strange when someone said I looked pretty. Now, I can say that I have healed from that.

Tools for rebuilding your children's self-esteem:

- If you have daughters, like in my case, have them participate in pageants/debutantes, fashion shows/ modeling, team-building exercises, etc. Also, you can have them participate in sports, school clubs, church youth groups, etc.

- Encourage them to write positive affirmations each day and hang them on the wall/mirror. Always remind them of how beautiful, valuable, and important they are to this world.
- Think positively, because when you think better, you do better.
- Give them a huge cheer for even the smallest successes. This helps to rebuild their confidence. Sometimes just hearing your parent say, "I'm proud of you," can mean the world to a child.
- Compliment them daily. This goes back to the positive affirmations. When they come from a parent, kids listen.
- Provide them with a safe environment, a place they're not afraid to share their feelings and be expressive.
- Always be conscious of what you say to your kids. During difficult times such as divorce, saying the smallest thing like, "No, not that one, silly," can affect a child. They are vulnerable, so always remember to be conscious and attentive to your child's needs.

Before we divorced, I googled Spiritual Groups for Separation, hoping to get help for me and my children, but was unable to find any support groups less than an hour away. I knew I needed help, but did not know how or where to get it. My church has ministries for singles, youths, women and married couples, but not one for those going through divorce or separation. So every Saturday, I again felt I did not belong anywhere. Joining a group to discuss, talk and share is very important because it allows you a place to have dialogue and get support from people that have been through what you're currently experiencing.

I'm always praying for my eldest daughter's spouse, because I don't want her to have to go through the pain of a divorce. I explain to her that what happened in my past relationships does not have to affect her relationship with her husband. My parents were blessed to be married for fifty-nine years. They had problems, but managed to always work it out. My difficulties in relationships were brought about because I was always running from something or someone, and not to God. I wish I knew half of the things back then that I know now. Wisdom is all we need to survive this thing called life!

Chapter 4

FINANCIAL INDEPENDENCE

*Honor the Lord with your wealth and with the first of all your crops.
Then your barns will be filled with plenty, and your vats will burst with wine.
(Proverbs 3:9-10-CEB)*

The state of my finances at the time of the divorce was challenging. I started out with a decent credit score during my marriage. However, my ex-husband did not have credit because of previous obligations that were not met in his past credit history, which meant we couldn't purchase anything in his name unless we wanted our interest rates to be extremely high. So, every account was put in my name while we were married. When we split up I was left with every debt that we ever created together including three houses, two cars, household accounts and credit card debt that we accrued over the years. Many days and nights, I wanted to give up, but with divine help and power I pushed through! I was able to get back in a good financial position.

Here are some key things that helped me to reestablish credit:

- Make a List of Checks / Balances.
- Identify where most of your money is being spent.
- Pay all accounts that have higher interest rates first.
- Once one account is paid off, use the money that was used to pay off that account for another account.
- Figure out ways you can save money.
- Pay your tithes each month.
- Pray and ask for wisdom concerning your finances.

This season in my life was very emotional. I was so embarrassed by everything. I felt I had to keep up a good appearance at all times and even continued doing some of the same things I did when there were two incomes in our homes. Can you imagine paying two car payments and three house payments with one salary? I can almost remember the exact penny of each monthly payment. The payments came around so fast that before I could breathe it was time to make another payment. My ex was able to take his clothes, car, and never look back. He never even considered helping with the bills.

I received all of the bill collection calls at home and work, which was another source of embarrassment for me. I always kept my family business private, so this made things even more challenging for me at work. Again, one of my biggest regrets was being so anxious to get the divorce that we did not include any property, antique furniture or cars in the agreement. I spoke with him several times about the deed to the house, but he always pushed it off by saying we would discuss it later. He really just wanted me to buy him out. He never made one payment or helped with anything financially during the closing of our house. Now, after being divorced for more than eight years, we finally returned to court to make this correction. This is another financial obligation for which I will be responsible. I refuse in this time and season of my life to pay him for not only cheating but also adding so many challenges to my children's lives.

Here are a few additional things that you should keep in mind when going through divorce:

- Who will provide the health insurance for your kids, if kids are involved?
- Consider the college fund for future education of the children.
- Consider tax filing.
- Consider car, Home Owner's, or Renter's Insurance.
- Consider credit card debt, if shared.
- Consider the phone bill, if shared.

You will need to make sure you have taken all of these things into consideration when going through divorce. Though they may sound minuscule, the cost can add up and really have an impact on your finances.

What I learned from this journey called divorce is to always pay your tithes and sow into good ground. Sowing into good ground can be accomplished by donating to a charity, helping a single mother who's trying to get back on her feet, etc. This provides preparation for you, so that when your rainy day comes, you will be able to endure. Even if you sow with just a little. We know God can turn little into much.

Also, always maintain your individual personal savings; not because you anticipate divorce but so that you're able to have a financial cushion in any situation. Be certain that the bills are spread out equally. If your spouse has bad credit, ensure they have a goal of working toward cleaning it up. Remember when you become one, that includes everything. We always want to be a help to each other and not be a burden. Otherwise, it could create tension in the marriage. You should *always* have a savings together, so that when the rainy days come you are financially prepared. So many people divorce this day in age because of their finances. I don't want any one marriage to become another statistic. Focus on building your credit, and make sure that everything is not in one person's name. On some occasions, you may need to wait to marry until you both are financially ready to avoid any additional hardships that may come up. Most importantly, always seek marriage counseling before getting married and discuss your finances and goals for your finances, to ensure that you are both on the same page.

Here is a Budget Spreadsheet to follow:

Monthly Budget Report

GOAL FOR THE MONTH			
OVERALL MONTHLY EXPENSES			
TOTAL SAVINGS			
EXPENSES	Goal for the month	Overall monthly expenses	Total savings
HOUSING			
TRANSPORTATION			
INSURANCE			
FOOD			
EDUCATION			
PERSONAL CARE			
PETS			
ENTERTAINMENT			
LOANS			
TAXES			
BANKING			
CHILDREN			
LEGAL			
TOTAL EXPENSES			

Hope, Healing, & Happiness After Divorce

Monthly Expenses: (Month)

HOUSING	Goal for the month	Overall Monthly Expenses	Total Savings	ENTERTAINMENT	Goal for the month	Overall Monthly Expenses	Total Savings
Mortgage or rent				Music/Video/DVD			
Cable				Dancing			
Phone				Movies			
Electricity				Concerts			
Gas				Social/Sporting Events			
Water and sewer				Arts/Crafts/Hobbies			
Other				TOTAL EXPENSES			
TOTAL EXPENSES				LOANS	Goal for the month	Overall Monthly Expenses	Total Savings
TRANSPORTATION	Goal for the month	Overall Monthly Expenses	Total Savings	Personal			
Vehicle payment				Credit card			
Bus/Taxi fare				Credit card			
Insurance				Credit card			
Fuel				Other			
Maintenance				TOTAL EXPENSES			
Other				TAXES	Goal for the month	Overall Monthly Expenses	Total Savings
TOTAL EXPENSES				Federal			
INSURANCE	Goal for the month	Overall Monthly Expenses	Total Savings	State			
Home				Local			
Health				Other			
Life				TOTAL EXPENSES			
Other				BANKING	Goal for the month	Overall Monthly Expenses	Total Savings
TOTAL EXPENSES				Checking			
FOOD	Goal for the month	Overall Monthly Expenses	Total Savings	Savings			
Groceries				Retirement account			
Dining out				Investment account			
Other				Other			
TOTAL EXPENSES				TOTAL EXPENSES			
EDUCATION	Goal for the month	Overall Monthly Expenses	Total Savings	CHILDREN	Goal for the month	Overall Monthly Expenses	Total Savings
Tuition				Child Support			
Books/Supplies				Babysitting			
Other				School Fees/Lunches			
TOTAL EXPENSES				Daycare/Afterschool			
PERSONAL CARE	Goal for the month	Overall Monthly Expenses	Total Savings	Savings Account			
Medical				School Supplies			
Hair/nails				TOTAL EXPENSES			
Clothing				LEGAL	Goal for the month	Overall Monthly Expenses	Total Savings
Health Club				Attorney/Legal Advisor			
Other				Alimony			
TOTAL EXPENSES				Court Fees			
PETS	Goal for the month	Overall Monthly Expenses	Total Savings	Counseling/Therapy			
Food				Other			
Supplies				TOTAL EXPENSES			
Medical							
Other							
TOTAL EXPENSES							

Chapter 5

HOPE AND HEALING

If my people, who are called by name, will humble themselves and pray and and seek my face and turn from their wicked ways, then I will hear from heaven, and I will forgive their sin and will heal their land.
(2 Chronicles 7:14-NIV)

Healing can be a long process. It could take months, sometimes years for a person to heal. There are several steps to the healing process. Divorce is sometimes referred to as a death in the family because of the absence of your spouse. But God allows everything in our lives to happen with purpose. He is drawing us closer to him when we're at our lowest point. He's right by our side through the entire journey. My Bishop often says "Even when you can not trace him, he's still there."

Here are a few steps to the healing process:

- Forgiveness
- Picking up the pieces
- God's message to us
- Remember, Love conquers all

- Church; my safe haven
- Strong values
- Counseling from Bishop

When I was able to see my ex-husband in person and realized I didn't have any feelings of bitterness or hostility, I knew I had forgiven him. Forgiveness was not for him but, more importantly, for myself. It helped me to pick up the pieces, learn from my mistakes, and move beyond my hurt. It's so important for us to stop and look at every experience in our lives and reflect on it. We learn many valuable lessons by reflecting. Always remember to stop, and listen to your heart so that you can learn from it and move on.

Love is a powerful thing; it conquers all when you're able to forgive and love someone beyond their faults. Unconditional love is not shared among many. What unconditional love means to me is to love someone without conditions. There's nothing they can do to make me stop loving them.

Church was a safe haven for me. It helped to ease my pain while going through this difficult time in my life. The gathering of the saints empowered me to continue to strengthen my faith and relationship with God. My strong Christian values promoted a source of healing for me. Also, counseling from my Bishop was important to ensure that the divorce was the right process for us. Dedication to the church helped rebuild my faith and allowed me not to ponder what was going on, but to focus on renewing my relationship with God.

Hope changes your perspective on any situation in which you may find yourself. It can give you the courage to pull through. It can serve as the guiding light to an unforeseen path. There is a treasure to be found in Hope. There are moments in our lives we feel there is no where to go but up. In those moments, I dig my heels in the ground and push my way through. We have all heard the phrase "let's hope for the best." Sometimes hoping for the best is just not enough. Many of you may have different belief systems. However, no matter your belief, we will all find that if you speak what you want enough, it will come to fruition. I'm a big believer in "Vision Boards." I created one and have since watched as those dreams and aspirations have taken a life of their own.

Without hope, I would have never created my vision board. Without hope, I can't say that I would have made it this far. It was the one thing that I clung onto through the entire divorce. I could only hope and pray that things would get better. I was at one of the darkest, and lowest moments of my life. I truly believed there was no where to go but up. It certainly could not get any worse. Or at least, that was my thought process, even before I realized that I was truly headed for divorce. I would hope and pray for a happy marriage, for unconditional love, for peace.

What Now?

Writing is a sense of therapy for me. Once I put something on paper it becomes real to me; I feel it really happened. Sometimes I feel so ashamed I cannot even put the words on paper. But even during the hard times, I try to write everyday. This helps me with my emotions. I've learned that I do not have to keep everything bottled up inside. When you bottle things up, eventually there comes an explosion.

Shopping and food have also been outlets for me, though not always healthy ones. It gave me comfort as I spent excessive amounts of money on food and clothing, using credit cards and personal loans. I enjoyed nice restaurants daily and gained a lot of weight because of it; when I get stressed, I tend to eat everything around me. Both of these spending habits caused financial burdens for me, because I was constantly spending money I did not actually have. I blamed my financial problems on my ex-husband, but I brought some of the struggles that existed into our marriage as well. I was not truly focused at that time, and I allowed my flesh to override everything I knew. I had a hard time concentrating on being a responsible single parent and prayed daily for deliverance in this area of my life.

We must learn to communicate and share our feelings with others. I asked God to guide me as to who I could share my personal information. We can't share our personal experiences with everyone. Sometimes people can't handle what you have done in your past or the things you are going through. My hope is that you will find elders or mature individuals in your life with whom to share your experiences.

Writing, shopping and eating have been, and at times continue to be, my escape. **However, I now look for help in this area of my life by doing other things like (not necessarily in this order):**

- Attending church functions
- Reading inspirational books
- Spending time daily with God through prayer
- Surrounding myself with people that love and support me

Scriptures in the Bible that have helped me in this season of my life are from the books of Psalms and Proverbs:

Psalms 46:1-NLT
"God is our refuge and strength, an ever-present help in trouble."

Psalms 106:1-NLT
"Praise the Lord. Give thanks to the Lord, for he is good; his love endures forever."

Psalms 124:8-NLT
"Our help is in the name of the Lord, the Maker of heaven and earth."

Proverbs 17:22-NLT
"A cheerful heart is good medicine, but a crushed spirit dries up the bones."

Proverbs 16:9-NLT
"In their hearts humans plan their course, but the Lord establishes their steps;"

Proverbs 16:7-NLT
"When the Lord takes pleasure in anyone's way, he causes their enemies to make peace with them."

Proverbs 18:21-NLT
"The tongue has the power of life and death, and those who love it will eat it's fruit."

I read scriptures daily to encourage my spirit. Today, I can say that I finally know who I am and to whom I belong. Whether you like or respect me, that is your choice. I know there are great things planned for me! Some things may be delayed in my life, but not denied. I continue to be blessed day-by-day through His grace and mercy.

Chapter 6

JOURNAL TO FREEDOM

Do not be anxious about anything, but in every situation, by prayer and petition, with thanksgiving, present your requests to God. (Philippians 4:6-7- NIV)

Journaling is a great way to share important events in your life as well as a way to relieve stress. Here are some of the journal entries I wrote while I was going through the different stages of my divorce process. It really helped me to deal with my emotions and balance my day-to-day activities. If I wrote it, the events were real to me. My thoughts were often scrambled in my mind when I was under a lot of stress, and writing them down helped to make things clearer for me.

I wrote my entries in beautiful journal books, subject books, on envelopes, napkins and whatever else I could find. Your books can be as fancy or plain as you would like them to be. Journal entries can be short or long depending on what's going on in your life at that point in time. The most important thing for you to do is just write. Here are some of the journal entries I wrote:

8/15/2008

I sit up in bed continuing to wonder about my future. My baby girl is growing so fast, so many questions. My eldest is still very protective over us because of all that has happened with my ex-husband. I pray that my baby girl's husband will be saved and God fearing. I pray for my church family in Jesus' name, Amen!

9/12/2008

I have not written in my journal in a while because I have been working on my 21-day projects (50 things). My life has been going fairly well. I often still wonder what I did wrong in my marriage. Some days I try to cover up the hurt. Lord, give me peace and strength to carry on in Jesus' name, Amen!

10/4/2008

What a busy blessed day! I went to a wedding today. The wedding was beautiful; I pray for them. I still wonder, "Why?" each day. Each day gets better with new tests and trials. What an awesome testimony I will have for someone else. I continue to give God the glory and honor in my life. I missed talking with Mom and Dad today. I will call them tomorrow.

10/13/2008

Oh, God, please help me and give me strength. God, I still miss my husband. I don't want to, but I do. Help me to let him go. I pray for my family, friends and my enemies in Jesus' name, Amen.

7/6/2009

I am still going through the divorce. When I come out of this, I know God has something great in store for me. No job yet—I applied in Halifax county and wrote an interest letter to another school. My youngest daughter still does not know what school she will be attending in the fall. God, please send me a gorgeous, saved, rich, God-fearing man (handsome, of course), who owns his own home and car. Someone I can talk to and confide in. Let me know whether or not I should let my marriage be dissolved, so I can move on. Help me and give me the words, your words, to tell my children how I feel.

Give me peace.

Let me know the plans you have for me.

In Jesus' name Amen!

God take away the loneliness!!!

I'm a big believer in writing down how I feel. This is a great source of expression for me, when trying to release pain, hurt, etc. I decided at this time in my life to write my ex-husband a letter. At this point, I was in a lot of pain from all of the things that had transpired in our marriage. I had internalized the infidelity, broken trust, disappointment, and so much more. It was all bottled up inside of me and I felt like this was a way for me to release some of it. The letter was for me; I had no intentions of giving it to him. It was my way of allowing self-expression for my own healing. I wrote the letter, then destroyed it. I was able to release some of the negativity that I was feeling toward him through this process.

It read:

Dear Husband,

I was very hurt by what you did to me. I love you and I respected you. We were the best of friends, not even discussing the covenant we made to each other. Best Friends! Best Friends! I invited you back in our lives several times but you always said, "Wait, give me more time," I guess to keep doing what you were doing. You allowed another woman to disrespect me by calling me and even coming to our home. You also allowed her to talk harshly to our children while I was still your wife. She sent you cards and stuffed animals to our home. You let them fall in my possession knowingly or unknowingly. She called and talked to me in the middle of the night and talked about your wonderful relationship. Of course, she shared with me about your beautiful little innocent angel that was a part of the two of you. She proceeded to tell me how overweight and no good I was to you. Now I leave you in the hands of the Lord. I forgive you, so I can go on in the Lord. I hope you will continue to have a father-daughter relationship with your two daughters.

Love,

Deborah

Please be careful and wise when journaling. It brings out a lot of emotions. Journals should be safe guarded; sometimes the people in your lives may really be offended by what is written. I have been journaling for years, and now I am debating whether to keep or destroy the journals. I do have them stored in one central location in my home. I believe that I am truly healed emotionally from past hurt in my life. I have ten journals, not including the many slips of dated paper and scraps. My youngest daughter told me she would like to read them, but I feel that these are some of my most precious and private thoughts. I guess I feel she may not understand some of my pain.

So you may find it necessary to shred or even burn these journals for closure as well. If journaling is the route you decide to take, be sure to consider the positive and negative results that may occur from your decision to journal. This can be a very emotional experience but also one that can provide much healing for you.

On the next pages you will see journal examples you can use if you are not sure how to begin your writing process. Feel free to add your own sections to make this more personal for you. However, this can create a start for you.

PRAYER JOURNAL

DATE: _____

Today I am thankful for: _____
_____
_____
_____

People to Pray for: _____
_____
_____
_____

Prayer Requests for Myself: _____
_____
_____
_____

Answered Prayers: _____
_____
_____
_____

PRAYER JOURNAL

DATE: _____

Today I am thankful for: _____
_____
_____
_____

People to Pray for: _____
_____
_____
_____

Prayer Requests for Myself: _____
_____
_____
_____

Answered Prayers: _____
_____
_____
_____

PRAYER JOURNAL

DATE: _____

Today I am thankful for: _____
_____
_____
_____

People to Pray for: _____
_____
_____
_____

Prayer Requests for Myself: _____
_____
_____
_____

Answered Prayers: _____
_____
_____
_____

Chapter 7

LOVING YOURSELF

I love you fervently and devotedly, O Lord, my Strength.
(Psalm 18:1-AMP)

Every negative thing that has ever been said to me comes back to mind because of the divorce. I truly believed what people said about me; back to being called "Miss Piggy" as a nickname. My spirit, feelings and emotions were really crushed for years because of pain from my childhood. So, no one can say that words don't hurt, because they really do. I am just now truly getting to know myself. Each day is a struggle, but I am confident that with God, I can love myself and allow others to love me to the fullest!

I believe that loving yourself is one of the most important things you can do, especially during a difficult time like divorce. How can you ever truly love another person if you don't even love yourself? As you begin, or continue, this new journey in your life, start to learn all you can about who you are. No longer focus on what happened to you in the past . . . Don't look back! My pastor often says "kiss your past goodbye." And that is what we are going to start working on in this chapter. Here are some things I would recommend to start learning more about who you are and to continue loving yourself:

- Take yourself out
- Go out with the girls or the guys
- Go to the movies or a play
- Get dressed up just because
- Buy a new outfit
- Go to a spa
- Have a game night; watch sports
- Read a few books
- Go for a long walk
- Get a manicure and pedicure
- Get a facial
- Treat yourself to a four/five-star restaurant

Remain within your financial budget, but be sure to treat yourself well, whatever that may mean for you. Make a list of some short and long term goals you would like to accomplish, then check items off as you complete each goal. This doesn't have to be an extensive list, but one you can have to give yourself an idea of where you can start. As you begin these activities, remember to be careful about getting advice from someone who has not experienced what you are going through. Many of your loved ones may want to help but don't have a clue of what you are really going through. This can cause you frustration and make it difficult to properly heal.

Loving Yourself

As I mentioned before, I write almost everyday. Not only for comfort, but as an outlet for my pain as well. Every stroke I make with my pen or pencil takes away some of the hurt and pain for me. I truly believe that you have to feel good about yourself to move forward in life or allow others in. Writing helps me to release the pain and embrace who I am, without shame or guilt.

My father taught me many years ago to recite the "Lord's Prayer" whenever I was nervous or concerned about anything going on in my life. To this day, I still recite the prayer because I know God will do just what He said He would do in His word.

As you learn how to love yourself, it is important to simply take time just to meditate on your day, week and month. Always have a place for where you want to go, and set a time for when you will do this. This not only gives you time for yourself, but it can also help you to relieve stress.

Exercising a few times a week can really help. Sometimes when you go for a long walk, once you return home, you forget what you were stressed out about before you began your walk.

I often tried to please people when I should have been focusing on myself with God. The people in my life still never saw who I really was. I was always trying to fit into a "precut model." I NEVER fit in! I cried and screamed, but in the end, I was still the same person in the eyes of others. I was trying to be who they wanted me to be. Until you realize who you truly are, it will never make a difference. I cannot be Miss_____ or Mrs._____ until I accept being

Deborah. Now I hold my head up high with God's grace and mercy in knowing who I am.

Some people will disappoint you and fail you every time. I've learned that people are not perfect; no matter how much confidence you put in them, they are not perfect. My girlfriend always says, "Never trust anyone with your whole heart, especially me." I never understood what she meant, until one day I wanted her to come over. She said she would not for reasons I may never know. I used to always put her on a level that was even too high for her to own up to. But today I believe she was trying to tell me that, "No one is perfect but our Father in Heaven."

I was in a service and the pastor said to "draw a picture of how you look." I held on to the tablet for months and never was able to draw a picture until about a month ago. Guess what! When I drew myself, I put tears on my oversized face. My perception of myself was not a positive one. But as time went on I added features of myself. Writing this book, I find myself growing positively, mentally, physically, and spiritually. Before, I would not even take photographs with family and friends, now I may even request a snap shot here or there (wink, wink)!!!

My Self Portrait

Try doing a self-portrait of yourself before and after reading this book.

Loving Yourself

—BEFORE—

—AFTER—

—SELF PORTRAIT—

Chapter 8

RESTORATION

"I will restore to you the years that the swarming locust has eaten, the hopper, the destroyer, and the cutter, my great army, which I sent among you. You shall eat in plenty and be satisfied, and praise the name of the Lord your God, who has dealt wondrously with you. And my people shall never again be put to shame."
(Joel 2:25-26 ESV)

Restoration can be defined by Merriam-Webster's online dictionary as "the act or process of returning something to it's original condition by repairing it, cleaning it, etc." When your heart has been shattered into pieces, no one here on earth understands the depth of your pain. It's not an easy process but I promise you there is a "light at the end of the tunnel."

Restoration takes place with a few fundamentals:

- Spiritual Restoration
- Mental Restoration
- Physical Restoration

Stress can affect your health and physical well being. My body was trying to tell me that it had reached its maximum and I didn't listen. I ended up in the hospital for seven days due to stress. I had severe migraine headaches. Turning on the lights or minuscule noise felt like torture. I didn't have an appetite for quite some time. Your family needs you, so it's important to restore yourself wholeheartedly. Our bodies will let us know when we have reached our stress maximum. Listen to your body. Don't push yourself beyond your body's mental and physical capacity.

Don't look at your current situation and think that life is over; rather know that it's just beginning. Although you may feel as though you're in the worst circumstances yet, don't ever lose sight of what's important and that's your belief system. "He will never leave you, nor forsake you."

Always look in the mirror and feel proud of what you see. You are beautiful! God created you perfectly! Sometimes I find myself in awe of God's creations. I may gently stroke my hand and imagine what He must have had in mind as he began creating us. He has so much love for us, that He took his time with every intricate detail for each and everyone of us. If you can imagine with me, He's the artist and we're the canvas. He gently strokes the canvas creating a priceless work of art. An original, no other can be found anywhere in the universe. Imagine that . . . He knows every hair on our head. Imagine the love and humility He must have felt as He created each of us.

Albert Einstein once said, "Look deep into nature, and then you will understand everything better." When you have time, go outside on one beautiful night and lie down on the grass and just look up at the stars and remember that there's life beyond the sky.

We will one day meet our Savior and there is joy to be found in that. Take in the air with a deep breathe and as you release just think of peace and serenity. We are sometimes so busy with all the responsibilities of our lives that we forget to "stop and smell the roses." Let's enjoy them.

We focus on helping everyone else; which is what we're called to do; but let's not get so busy that we forget to help ourselves. Take time to sit back and reflect on all the great, miraculous things that have happened in your life. Remember those tough trials that you made it through in the past. A way of escape was provided then, and it will be the same for you now. There is beauty in pain, and remember, nothing happens by chance. "And we know that all things work together for the good to those who love God," (Romans 8:28-NKJV).

Some of the ways to practice the fundamentals of Restoration include:

Spiritual Restoration

- Find a quiet, open space to relax and concentrate on 3 things that had an impact on your life today. Don't label positive or negative, just find a balance between all things. Focus and meditate on those things and remember to give thanks for everything.
- Don't put high expectations on any one person. Accept people as they are.

Mental Restoration

- Understand and take responsibility for your choices.
- Do not battle within your thoughts. Make a decision and either amend or stick with it.

Physical Restoration

- Differentiate between what feels good for the time-being and what will feel even better in the long term.
- Actively review your short and longterm goals until progress occurs or completion.

Chapter 9

MOVING FORWARD/ DATING AGAIN

I waited patiently for the Lord, and he inclined unto me, and heard my cry.
(Psalm 40:1- KJV)

After the healing and restoration process, you finally get to a place where you are ready to move forward with your life. You learn to accept things for what they are and to move on. It's so important to have a great support system around you, including family and friends. It was vital for me to remain active. **Here are a few ways how:**

- Attending social events
- Attending family events
- Doing things that I enjoy and that keep me busy, like sewing, yoga, crafting, fishing, or book club.

I spent time with my children, and tried to demonstrate to them that when life throws you a curve ball you have to get back up again. Face whatever your mountain may be and tell that mountain to move. Don't allow it to hinder you, or hold you hostage.

Also, I made sure that I was on track financially so that I could provide a great future for my girls.

Most importantly, I began my new life with God first and foremost. I didn't want to continue living traditions, but I wanted to have a relationship with Him. My new church helped me to bring about a change within myself. When God lives within you, people around you will notice. There is something different about you, people will say. You have a peace that only He can give you.

I now know and understand my value. I no longer want to live up to everyone's expectations except God's plan. Sometimes we want to focus on all of the things in life that are going wrong, but we should try focusing on everything that is going right. Have faith in the plan for your life. Therefore, don't worry or fret about the things that are going on around you. We are being shaped into the individuals that we are to be with every obstacle that comes our way. I thank God that he gave me the strength and wisdom to move forward in such a time as this.

You are right where you are supposed to be at this very moment. Don't question it, yet embrace it, and live in the present. Don't ponder on the past, but understand your past doesn't define you. It's just a part of your story!

DATING AGAIN

Here are a few tips for dating again:

- Be open, warm, and intriguing, but most importantly, be yourself.
- It's okay to talk about yourself, but don't share everything all at once.
- Don't do all of the talking.
- Don't talk about your ex; this is a big "No, No."
- Be conscious of the location you choose to meet (I recommend a nice restaurant, Starbucks, Barnes and Noble, etc.). Be conscious of the noise level at the location you choose, so that you can hear each other clearly.
- Even if the date doesn't go well, be sure to thank them for their time.
- Practice abstinence. He or she should realize your value and understand you're worth the wait.
- Make sure the second date (if you have one) is somewhere fun. This way you get to see him or her in a different element.
- Be attentive and listen carefully.

Remember, you have to always be true to who you are when dating. This is why it is very important to heal first. Often times, people are afraid to allow someone to see their true selves. However, I would encourage this because it's important to reveal your true identity–always. If this person ends up being your partner for life, you want them to know exactly what they are getting; just as you would want to know. Also, remember, "A man who findeth a wife findeth a good thing." It's a great feeling to be loved.

It was interesting to begin dating again after being married for so long. However, it was a process. The first gentleman I dated right after my divorce really helped me to be at ease and take my mind off of things. However, I realized that a longterm relationship would not be our destiny.

One Sunday at church, I met this really nice gentleman. We exchanged phone numbers and began talking over the phone for about four months. The next step was our first date, at a local place in our home town. Instantly, there was a connection between the two of us. I was hesitant about bringing any man around my daughter. I did not want to expose her to men that would not be in our life for the long haul. She had been through so much pain already. However, this man was different.

Here are a few things to look for in new relationships:

- The person is intelligent and knows how to communicate.
- The person is emotionally invested.
- The person is apologetic when he/she should be (hopefully he/she doesn't have too much to apologize for at this point). A person can always say the words "I'm sorry" but does he/she really mean it? Ask yourself that.
- The person has a great sense of humor.

God has a funny way of working in a person's life. Months before my book (this book to be exact) was finished, I met this wonderful young man. Talk about surprises! He treats me like a queen. He is a family man, loves me dearly and always has my best interest in the forefront of his mind. We both had been hurt because of the ones we chose to love. Hurt people tend to hurt others. We vowed to break this pattern and decided to get married and spend the rest of our lives together. If ever one decides to move on, consult a counselor, who knows, loves, and fears the Lord. Someone who will help you release that baggage and not carry it into your next relationship. Lastly, remember to include God, because a marriage really takes three. We also agreed to receive additional counseling after our marriage for the next year.

My pastor married us. We had a beautiful wedding ceremony with a few family members and friends that would embrace our new start together in this thing called "Life."

When I say I received truly what I asked for, that is exactly what I mean! We have been married now for four years. I would be lying if I told you everyday has been a "bed of roses." But I can say we both love on the Lord daily, and ask God regularly to lead and guide us through our marriage. Disagreements only last short periods of time, and then we are ready again to keep moving on. He is truly a family man, showing himself to be worthy of this over and over again. We are not perfect by any means, but we are striving to be daily in Jesus' name.

I will admit that I am one who is still afraid to let anyone "love" me fully. It is so scary. I don't want him to hold my hand or kiss me in public. I am afraid of being embraced. He deals with this daily, but has continued to love me anyway and even encouraged me to write this book. He does so many things for my daughter and me. I can't even begin to name them all. I thank God for sharing him with me in this season and place in my life. Even as I look at our marriage, I see that He may not come when you want Him to, but He is always on time!

I feel that it is necessary for mothers or mature believers of the church to talk with the young women about marriage and dating. We often let this wisdom go to waste by not tapping into it. My dream is to counsel divorced women, especially due to infidelity. Many women hold this information of hurt inside while layers of bitterness and unwillingness to forgive build up.

If you have a relationship with God, He will help you to go through this season of your life. I really did expect my marriages to be "until death do us part." I often wonder what would have happened if I stayed and remained unhappy. I do really believe that once you are married, you should try to make it work. God ordained marriage. You must also remember you can not make an adult obey. Are you equally yoked? If not, that is your first struggle. In general, remember that struggles come to make you strong. This test is really not for you, it is for someone else. A Testimony! Wow! Isn't that something!

Chapter 10

JOYFUL LIVING

For I know the thoughts that I think toward you, saith the Lord, thoughts of peace, and not of evil, to give you an expected end.
(Jeremiah 29:11- KJV)

Joyful living is up to you. We must be appreciative of what we have and where we are in life. Happiness doesn't come from material things, it comes from within. Always remember to live in the present. Take time to focus on the positive inspirations in your life. Here are a few positive inspirations to help you in joyful living:

- Make sure your home is a safe haven,
- Surround yourself with things you love (i.e. pets, books, music, etc.),
- Laugh out loud,
- "Dance in the rain, snow,"
- Keep positive friends in your inner circle,
- Tell family and friends that you love them every chance you get,
- Remember every moment in life is important and make it count,
- Be a life long learner, knowledge is power.

Joyful living can reduce stress and enable you to live a healthy, happy, lifestyle. Often times we can be our own worst enemy in applying these tools. We are our hardest critic. With that said, you may wonder . . .

How are things in my new relationship with my ex? Well, we are still not where we should be, but I thank goodness we are not where we used to be either. Once I truly forgave myself, I was finally able to forgive him. Believe me, that was a process! For now, we still communicate through my daughters. I try to remain open-minded, but sometimes it is still a trying struggle. I feel my family doesn't see my hurt in all of this. It's hard when you have been with someone for so long. Both of your families grow close to one another. I cried as I wrote this, because I remembered how I felt at that time. I felt my family wasn't supportive of me in the way that I needed them to be during the divorce process. They couldn't understand my decisions to divorce, and I felt they constantly took his side. My mother was in a nursing facility for more than four years and yet she never, ever failed to ask me how he was doing. Although this was painful, I always thought of something positive to say about him and his new family. After all, he wasn't some horrible person. He was someone who was hurt. Remember that hurt people hurt others. We were the best individuals we knew how to be at that time.

I continue to encourage our baby girl to keep her father informed on what's going on with her life. My prayer is that they continue to strengthen their relationship, spend more time together, and have unconditional love for one another no matter what. Always try to maintain a relationship with your ex if there are children involved. This is so important for the kids.

I am grateful I was able to go through and move beyond this difficult process in my life. My baby girl is now eighteen years old and in her first year in college. No more child support. It gets hard sometimes but, I know I can do anything my mind can imagine. If I hadn't gone through this process where would I be? I wouldn't be the person I am today. Maybe I wouldn't have written this book. So, I say, thank you!

The key to joyful living is to accept things for what they are. Remember that nothing happens by chance. God knew that you were strong enough to endure this situation. I try to find joy in everything; even the simplest of things. The joy in this situation is that my kids are healthy and well. My ex-husband is healthy and well. During this season I learned so much. There were little drops of wisdom that he either dropped in my spirit or that I dropped in his. I learned that trust isn't given, it's earned. I also learned to quiet my spirit, along with all the background noise, and to humble myself. Joy is given each and every day you wake up. You determine the feelings you hold inside. Whether it be happiness, joy, bitterness, etc. Today and everyday, let's chose JOY! It resides within you. God is the joy of my heart and soul. Most importantly, through this process I learned the power of forgiveness!

Chapter 11

WHAT ACTUALLY CAUSED OUR DIVORCE? AND HOW TO AVOID IT

How can you say to your brother, 'Brother, let me take the speck out of your eye,' when you yourself fail to see the plank in your own eye? You hypocrite, first take the plank out of your eye, and then you will see clearly to remove the speck from your brother's eye.'
(Luke 6:42- NIV)

One day, I was having a conversation with a friend. During this conversation, my friend completely belittled my marriage. To make it worse, she has never been divorced or been in a similar situation. This hurt very much; as I'm sure it would've hurt anyone. It reminds me to always be careful when giving advice on a problem or obstacle I haven't experienced myself, because it can unintentionally hurt someone a lot more than help them. Yes, it is good to sometimes let a person you trust and respect be your listening ear, regardless of their experience in the subject; however, you also don't want to share information with someone that will make you feel small as a person. Divorce is already difficult enough and you don't need to be around people that will tear you down, even if they don't mean to do so.

Now what does this actually have to do with why my husband and I were getting divorced? Well, as much as my friend's words hurt, I truly believed that my marriage was still a sacred union at one time in my life. But I also knew that marriage depended on all parties involved. So I began to do some self-reflection on the root causes of our marriage issues.

After some long and difficult reflection, these were some of the main issues I found in our marriage. I think you may be able to relate to some of these points as well.

1. Lack of communication
2. Money management and financial roles
3. God not being the head of our marriage (Most important!)
4. Commitment issues and lust
5. Honesty and trust
6. Covering up problems
7. Relationship priorities
8. I was always afraid to be happy

I took a huge financial role in our marriage, which was another big mistake. The man should be the head of the household. Sometimes I feel that his not being head of the household contributed to his double life. Depending on what situation you may be in, responsibilities should or can go toward the higher income. Make sure it's a team effort; this keeps an open line of communication.

My ex began coming home very late at night and leaving extremely early the next morning. I was not so suspicious at first due to the type of work he did. My ex had several affairs before we were married. Therefore, there was always a trust issue with me. Even when he was not doing anything, I often accused him of committing adultery because of our past.

One night he came in extremely late and I waited up patiently for him in our living room. He always knew I was a hard sleeper and would not know the time he came in other than it was after midnight. When he entered the door, the argument began. I told him how I felt, that I was suspicious of his behavior, and he basically said, "Get out of my face, I am an adult." After an hour of screaming and crying I went into my prayer language. It scared him and I was terrified because this had never happened to me before. This got his attention. He did everything in his power to calm me down by hugging and embracing me while we sat in the middle of our hallway floor. The children fortunately never woke up because their bedrooms were upstairs in our house. I never used my prayer language again until about ten years later.

Our marriage went on fine for many years, then, all of a sudden, the same types of things happened again, late arrivals, earlier departures, gifts for him with no cards attached, items being hidden. This time I gave him an ultimatum of leaving or staying. He thought he did not have to make a decision, but I was persistent about him making a decision.

A few weeks later, I left for a couple of days for a school conference. I called him while I was driving and asked him to be gone when I returned if he was going to continue this type of behavior. He did not say what he would do on the telephone. When I returned, I am sad to say he was gone; he had made a decision. After he left, I still was not sleeping but eating all I could while he was on his wild adventures. Trying to teach at school was very challenging. I often avoided my co-workers as much as possible. I put all of my energy into loving and teaching my students that were assigned to me that year. I even stopped paying attention at home with my girls, not even realizing it until the oldest expressed how much attention I was giving my job and not my family. I was really hurting and hurting my daughters in the process. I hope they can and have forgiven me for my shortcomings through that long and drawn out separation and divorce. I am truly sorry for any hurt or pain that I caused them while growing up. We as a family always had food, clothing and shelter, but the most important piece that we didn't always get right was the unconditional love piece. I still loved my ex no matter what he had done, said to me or said about me.

On top of everything else, during this rough time in our marriage, I had horrible dreams about my husband entertaining other women. I had this same dream over and over, night after night, week after week. I was so ashamed, hurt, and felt betrayed by my "Best Friend." I spoke with my ex about my dreams and he would often say I was being silly and emotional. I would tear up at almost anything at that time. I finally spoke with a dream interpreter and he stated, "The dream meant God wanted to be in a closer relationship with me during that season." The dreams stopped for a while after we separated but returned again. I had those dreams off and on even after the divorce. I finally took the interpreter's advice and started reading my word, praying more and building a relationship with God. I guess that is where my true healing started to take place.

Think of people that you know who are married, the ones that are truly happy and successful in their marriage. What was the order of their marriage? Husband and wife together, then children? Or is there a different order? Is God first in their lives? Did the woman find the man? Is the man truly the head or is the woman carrying the man's duties as the head? Most women pray to one day get married, have children and live in a beautiful home. However, we can sometimes become too anxious for our time, not realizing that it may not be the season or even the plan for our lives.

Society often has input on what they see with the natural eye. But what often seems perfect can be merely an outside show. When making comments, we must remember that all humans sometimes fall short. My struggle has been in the area of forgiveness. People do not realize how they often affect not only you but also others that are connected to you. Years later, I still struggle with decisions I have made that will affect me the rest of my life. Let's think of the "Lord's Prayer." You must forgive yourself as well as others in your life. When a person asked me to pray for someone in my past, I truly thought that I had forgiven the person because it happened years ago, but it was still there just under layers where I tucked it away.

As you can see, divorce can be a very painful process. After going through a divorce as well as recently marrying again, I wanted to share some tips to not only prevent divorce but to help you with your next relationship. Here are five essentials you should implement in order to prevent divorce. Let's stop and focus on ways we can avoid it, if at all possible.

Tips for Preventing Divorce

1. TIME MANAGEMENT: PUT TIME AND EFFORT INTO YOUR MARRIAGE

My husband and I pick one day of the week that we call "our time," with no interruption from others, including family and friends. Sometimes we may plan to go out (bowling, movies, plays), other times we just stay home and watch TV or take time for conversation with each other. This is just as we did before we were married. We also plan activities with our close friends. Girls Night Out! Guys Watching Games! We feel the need to spend time apart sometimes, with other important people in our lives, as absence makes the heart grow fonder. We realize how blessed we are to have each other and how much we really love each other. It's important for me to take time to reflect on our marriage and always remember why I fell in love with him. We also plan a yearly anniversary trip. We take turns doing what the other enjoys doing. This year it is his turn. Remember, you get out of the marriage whatever you put in it.

2. STAY IN THE WORD

Attend a Bible-based church and study your word daily. I often read devotionals and inspirational books. My husband really enjoys reading out of a bible with different versions. My dad always said there must be three things constant in your marriage, which are love, respect, and trust. Many wedding ceremonies have taken out portions of the vows to relinquish the commitment. Marriage is a covenant. Don't throw in the towel or fall into the many traps

Satan will set before you to tempt you. We sometimes think the grass is greener on the other side. Remember, Satan will test your marriage in areas where he knows you are weak. Sometimes, just stop and pray.

3. COMMUNICATION IS THE KEY

Every morning before we depart from each other, we leave with a kiss and say the words "I love you!" to each other. The three little words are very powerful. Right away, we both can tell how each is feeling by these small gestures. Listening to your spouse is very important. It reassures that the person feels heard. We discuss our disappointments; they happen as well. But most importantly, we talk about our happy moments or milestones. We are willing to compromise. Even when we argue, we are willing to talk about it shortly thereafter, in an effort not to hurt one other. I love that about my husband most of all. He was telling his friend about our relationship and his friend shared that he and his wife would drag out their arguments for days. Therefore, we are blessed in the sense that we are able to share our feelings and move on. We did discuss the importance of keeping certain information confidential as it pertains to our household. One of my biggest pet peeves is when husbands and wives try to embarrass each other in public. We talk and discuss the gifts we give each other. Sometimes we really need to be honest about what each other truly wants and what we want each other to have. We set goals and desires for our marriage. This allows us to work on areas that are weak/strong in our marriage.

4. MONEY

A great concern in many marriages is the finances. We must remember, what is his is mine and what is mine is his. As a couple, you must set up a process to handle the finances of the household. The spouse that is most financially responsible is usually the one who ensures all financial responsibilities of the family. Other questions to be considered: Will there be a joint checking and saving account? How much coverage will we need for life insurance policies? Will we split the bills or will there be a joint account in which all bills will be paid? etc. My husband and I now have a limited amount that can be spent on large purchases and we must consent with each other prior to purchasing.

We decided to take a trip each year. So we fill a coin jar from August to August to offset the cost. This has been fun and a great source of monies to be used for different things on trips. The key is not to touch the jar.

The money topic should be discussed well before the marriage at counseling sessions.

5. INTIMACY

Lastly, you must remember that most women are emotional creatures and some men are not. Therefore as women we must learn to deal with and adjust our attitudes. Calm down, take a deep breath, do not blow everything out of proportion. Remember to smile, laugh more and enjoy each other. It takes less muscle use to smile, than to frown. Men desire physical contact more often than most women. We must learn to love one another unconditionally. Never go to sleep angry and always find a way to move past your hurt. It should be an honor to be intimate with your spouse. This is one of the most important ways we can connect and demonstrate our love for one another.

Chapter 12

GOALS FOR THE FUTURE

For with God nothing shall be impossible.
(Luke 1:37 KJV)

I now try to write down goals that I want to accomplish in the next year, three years, and even five years. This helps me stay focused. I write all of this in a journal and check off goals as they are completed.

I went to a church one night and the Bishop talked about people getting items off of your "shelf," so to speak. He referenced that some people in your life get what they need off of your "shelf" and put back what they do not want. What I believe he was trying to share with us is that people can sometimes use you to get what they want. He referred to our different gifts and talents and how some people can take advantage of them. He talked about how well each of us knows ourselves, so why not write about ourselves? This created a great way for us to explore our talents and make use of them ourselves. So, I began writing daily about myself and wow! I found out so much about myself. I ended up with a small book of items about myself that I could publish as well. Some items included "My 50 Best Scriptures," "How Can I Please God?" etc. This small book with over twenty pages tells the real story about me (MY LIFE). As I read it, I tend to scratch off things that are no longer important to me and things I plan to accomplish. How powerful!

Here is an example of my goal sheet: Deborah Durham

MONTHLY GOAL SHEET COMPLETION DATES:

GOALS	IN PROGRESS	COMPLETED
Write and publish my book May 2015		X
Take Bible Classes Ongoing	X	
Spend More Time In Prayer Daily	X	
Read a Book Monthly	X	
Get a Full Time or Part Time Job		X
Lose 5 pounds Monthly	X	

Goals For The Future

NOTES:

RESOURCES NEEDED:
Books /Money /Pens/Pencils
Paper/ Scale/ Bible

MONTHLY GOAL SHEET COMPLETION DATES:

GOALS	IN PROGRESS	COMPLETED

Goals For The Future

NOTES:

Chapter 13

CLOSING

Confess your faults one to another, and pray one for another, that ye may be healed. The effectual fervent prayer of a righteous man availeth much. (James 5:16 KJV)

I wrote this book because I had searched and searched to find literature or books on divorce. I never could really find what I needed. Hopefully, this will help you as much as it helped me writing it. It was very therapeutic. No circumstance or situation is too hard for God. Ask God to help you make wise decisions, to give you as my Bishop says, "Spiritual Antennas." When you make a wrong decision out of emotional responses, as we often do, "God will put us back on the right track." It may take some time, but he'll do it. He will also give us revelation of His word if we would only ask Him to.

Now just sit back, pray, continue your relationship with the Master and see what your beautiful future holds. Fill your heart, mind, and soul with peace, joy, happiness, love and comfort.

Chapter 14

DIVORCE MANUAL

In their hearts humans plan their course, but the Lord establishes their steps.
—Proverbs 16:9

This Divorce Manual is included to note valuable tools and resources when contemplating or going through divorce. I hope the information covered below will be helpful to you. Now let's begin.

In General, here are a few "tell-tale" signs that may allude to the fact that your marriage is heading for divorce:

Often times your spouse will show signs of having extramarital affair(s). Signs may include your spouse telling you the following: "I have to work late", "that's just someone from work calling" (as they will not answer the call in front of you).

If you are constantly bickering with your spouse that could possibly be a sign. Sometimes your spouse may start an argument to give them a reason to leave the house.

If you continually contemplate divorce, this can also be a sign. You may constantly think about what your life would be like without your spouse.

When you begin sleeping in separate beds that is almost always the beginning of the end, in my opinion.

If you find yourself relating to many of the scenarios listed above, it's time to truly put all of your focus on your marriage and give it your biggest effort if you can. I understand that some marriages are just unsalvageable.

The process of deciding to divorce is no cake walk. Once you have begun the process, it will be an emotionally draining process as you can imagine.

No one has lived or experienced marriage through your eyes. Therefore, don't seek out the approval of family and friends. Be confident in your decision. Otherwise, you will stay on an emotional roller coaster.

Accept support from those who are genuine, whom you trust, and most importantly, who have a relationship with God.

The Legal Process is not something anyone looks forward to when going through divorce.

Gather all legal documents and resources you will need to proceed with the divorce.

Get an appraisal of property and/or anything you own. What are your assets? If you need money for divorce, can you liquidate your assets? What about savings for your child's future? What about any shared accounts you have (what to do with that money)?

My recommendation is to hire a divorce attorney. Have them file a petition for divorce. Request alimony, child support, and community property when necessary. Don't be afraid to be proactive in your financial state and ensure a bright future for yourself and especially for your kids, if they are involved. If there is joint property, both parties will have to negotiate on who will be awarded the property. Often times, individuals may "buy out" the other individual's name on the deed.

Visitation rights and privileges. Share "joint custody" when possible, so that you can keep things as normal as possible for the kids. You can also check with your lawyer to find out if you can put a clause in the divorce decree that includes making sure the children are not around your ex's new significant other, in order to ensure the safety of the child both physically and emotionally.

My Prayer is that you will have an Uncontested Divorce. Which is "a divorce proceeding in which the parties have reached an agreement on all issues."

After the divorce, it is not easy but remember that the marriage wasn't healthy for you.

Make sure you have a plan in place for your new future. Meditate and Pray every day. This is so important. You will really need to hear from God during this time for wisdom and guidance. Parents should present a unified front to their kids. The worse thing you can do is put your kids in the middle by speaking negatively about your ex in front of them. Don't make your child feel bad for wanting to spend time with your ex. Listen to your child and try to keep as much normalcy as possible. Continue to keep a journal, notating the entire process to date. Remain active by going out with friends, family, to church, etc. Most of us tend to get a serious makeover after a big change in our lives. If you decide to do this, have fun and enjoy the new you!

OVERVIEW

Deborah's Journey

1. What is your story? Write it down and allow this to be a form of therapy for you. Be sure to keep it in a safe place or throw it away afterwards.

_____

_____

_____

_____

_____

_____

_____

_____

_____

_____

_____

_____

_____

_____

_____

2. What is your testimony? There is a message in every story; understand your message so that you can be a blessing to others when they are going through life's hardships.

The Divorce

1. What was your takeaway regarding divorce in this chapter?

2. What is your definition of a happy marriage?

Voice of the Children

1. Identify strategies and activities to help kids cope with divorce.

2. Make a list of counselors; go through and find one that is suitable for your child's personality.

_____

_____

_____

_____

_____

_____

_____

_____

_____

_____

_____

_____

_____

_____

Financial Independence

1. Explore companies that specialize in helping individuals get back on their feet financially. Make a list and identify the one that can help you the most.

_____

_____

_____

_____

_____

_____

_____

_____

_____

_____

_____

_____

_____

2. Refer to the financial spreadsheet in chapter 4; create a budget that reflects going from two incomes to now one. If you're single and thinking about marriage, create a spreadsheet that reflects just the opposite; going from one income to two. You will need to know your fiancé's current salary.

Hope and Healing

1. Make a list of inspirational quotes that focus on forgiveness. Post them on your refrigerator or mirror and repeat them daily.

_____
_____
_____
_____
_____
_____
_____
_____
_____
_____
_____
_____
_____
_____
_____
_____
_____

2. Make a list of everything you learned from your divorce and identify how those things can help you grow.

_____
_____
_____
_____
_____
_____
_____
_____
_____
_____
_____
_____
_____
_____
_____

Journal to Freedom

1. Purchase a journal if you don't already have one, and begin today with a positive affirmation.

_____
_____
_____
_____
_____
_____
_____
_____
_____
_____
_____
_____
_____
_____
_____
_____

2. Include an affirmation and meditate on it daily.

Loving Yourself

1. What is the definition of "Love" to you?

_____

_____

_____

_____

_____

_____

_____

_____

_____

_____

_____

_____

_____

_____

_____

_____

_____

2. No one can treat you better than you can treat yourself. Explore different places where you can go on a retreat and pamper yourself. Be sure to include all options.

_____

_____

_____

_____

_____

_____

_____

_____

_____

_____

_____

_____

_____

_____

_____

_____

Restoration

1. Spend an hour each morning talking to God.

2. Begin putting together food regimens that provide energy and nutrients needed to live a healthy life.

Moving Forward / Dating Again

1. Make a note of the tools necessary for you at this point in your life to rebuild your future. Think about what you have overcome and write down where you would like to be in the future.

_____

_____

_____

_____

_____

_____

_____

_____

_____

_____

_____

_____

_____

2. Structure is key. Start by filling your calendar with activities right away.

3. Write down all of the qualities you would like in a spouse.

4. Purchase a new outfit and make sure you're always dressed to impress. You never know who's watching.

Joyful Living

1. Always make a conscious effort with your ex. No excuses. Try to think of a nice gesture you can apply when you see him. Remember, forgiveness is more for you than it is for your ex.

2. Write a letter and include all of the things you are grateful for in your life.

_____

_____

_____

_____

_____

_____

_____

_____

_____

_____

_____

_____

_____

_____

_____

What Caused Our Divorce? And How To Avoid It

1. Make a list of what caused your divorce.

_____

_____

_____

_____

_____

_____

_____

_____

_____

_____

_____

_____

_____

_____

_____

_____

_____

2. What are some preventative measures you can put in place to try to not end up in divorce again?

___

Goals For The Future

1. Refer to the goal sheet in chapter 12. Make sure that you're realistic when setting your goals.

_____

_____

_____

_____

_____

_____

_____

_____

_____

_____

_____

_____

_____

_____

_____

_____

_____

2. Follow up within a month's time to ensure you're on track with reaching your goals.

_____
_____
_____
_____
_____
_____
_____
_____
_____
_____
_____
_____
_____
_____
_____

Closing

1. What did you learn from this book?

_____
_____
_____
_____
_____
_____
_____
_____
_____
_____
_____
_____
_____
_____
_____
_____
_____

2. In a year's time, be sure to do some self-reflection to monitor your growth.

Resources

Holy Bible: King James Version

Google.com—Brainy Quotes: Reinhold Niebur

Biblegateway.com
New American Standard Bible (NASB)
Common English Bible (CEB)
New International Version (NIV)
Amplified Bible (AMP)
English Standard Version (ESV)
Merriam-Webster's Online Dictionary

Quote: Albert Einstein pg. 58

McQuade, Pamela L. the Bible Search Engine.
Barbour Publishing, 2011.

Pfeiffer, Charles F. The New Combined Bible Dictionary and Concordance.
Baker Book House. 1961.

New Living Translation (NLT), Version Information BibleGateway.com

Legal terms:
http://www.divorcehq.com/divorce-terminology.shtml

http://family-law.lawyers.com/divorce/words-and-terms-you-should-know-divorce-and-family-law.html

Psychology terms:
http://www.divorcemed.com/Articles/ArticlesByDiane/The%20Psychological%20Stages%20of%20Divorce.htm

http://www.mediate.com/articles/saporo.cfm

http://www.mediate.com/articles/psych.cfm

About the Author

Deborah Durham is a resident of Henderson, NC. She is married to James Durham and they have six daughters. Deborah has two Masters Degrees in Education and Administration. She prides herself in working hard to help serve others. Deborah is a retired teacher. She was second Runner Up for Teacher of the Year in Warren County. She was also recognized as an A+ Employee in Granville County. She is a National Board Certified Teacher and passionate about the education of the children. She leads with the philosophy that every child can be who they desire to be if they just believe in themselves. She is also a minister at Fresh Anointed Tabernacle of Deliverance in Henderson, NC. Deborah is currently attending Hidden Manna Bible College and Faith Landmarks Bible College. Deborah serves as the leader for Greeters Ministry, and Praise Dance Ministry. She enjoys reading inspirational books, teaching, and being active in the church. This is her first of many book projects. She is a giver at heart and enjoys helping others and hopes that this book will serve as a platform to help the wounded and broken hearted.

For book signing, engagements, seminars/workshops:

Email: booking.deborahjean@yahoo.com

www.ingramcontent.com/pod-product-compliance
Lightning Source LLC
Chambersburg PA
CBHW070625300426
44113CB00010B/1664